Glimpses of Heaven

Poems and Prayers
of mystery and wonder

Written and compiled
by Lois Rock

A LION BOOK

To Margaret Dean for her wisdom and inspiration

Compilation copyright © 1997 Lois Rock
This edition copyright © 1997 Lion Publishing
Illustrations copyright © 1997 Gabrielle Izen
Photography by John Williams Studios, Thame
Pottery on p.35 by Fowey Pottery

Published by
Lion Publishing plc
Sandy Lane West, Oxford, England
ISBN 0 7459 3632 6
Albatross Books Pty Ltd
PO Box 320, Sutherland, NSW 2232, Australia
ISBN 0 7324 1487 3

First edition 1997
10 9 8 7 6 5 4 3 2 1 0

Acknowledgments
p.18 'Sing to us, Mama…' copyright © Fan Tew Yeng, first published in
Aliran Monthly
p.21 'My Mother's Name is Worry' from Reading the Bible as Asian
Women, copyright © Christian Conference of Asia.
p. 23 'Sadness' copyright © Laura Braithwaite

A catalogue record for this book is available
from the British Library

Printed and bound in Singapore

From the Bible
Scriptures quoted or adapted from the Good News Bible published by
the Bible Societies/HarperCollins Publishers Ltd UK © American Bible
Society, 1996, 1971, 1976, 1992 unless otherwise stated.

p.7 A great mystery: Job chapter 38, verses 6, 8 and 18
p.9 Look at the flowers: Matthew chapter 6, verses 28 to 30;
The world's song: Psalm 148, especially verses 1 and 9 to 12
p.11 A harvest song: Psalm 65, especially verses 1 and 9 to 13
p.13 Let the favour of the Lord our God…: Psalm 90, verse 17, from the
New Revised Standard Version of the Bible, copyright 1989 by the
Division of Christian Education of the National Council of the Churches
of Christ in the USA
p.15 One prayer only: Psalm 27, verses 4 and 5
p.19 Jesus was speaking…: Matthew chapter 5, verses 43 and 44
p.21 I look at the high hills…: Psalm 121, verses 1 to 3;
God says this…: Isaiah chapter 61, verse 8
p.23 God asks a question: Job chapter 38, verses 34, 37 and 38 and
chapter 42, verses 1 to 6
p.25 Dear God…: Psalm 51, verses 1 to 2 and 11;
Jesus said, 'You can be sure of this…': Luke chapter 15, verse 7;
Jesus said, 'If you forgive…': Matthew chapter 6, verse 14
p.27 Hear my prayer…: Psalm 55, verses 1 to 4;
My God…: Psalm 22, verse 1
p.31 Long ago: Isaiah chapter 9, verses 2 and 6;
Jesus said, 'I am the light…': John chapter 8 verse 12
p.33 One evening…: John chapter 13, verses 1 to 16 and 34;
Jesus said, 'Peace…': John chapter 14, verse 27
p.35 Jesus and the Last Supper: Matthew chapter 26, verses 26 to 30;
Mark chapter 14, verses 22 to 26; Luke chapter 22, verses 14 to 20;
1 Corinthians chapter 11, verses 23 to 25
p.37 Jesus was betrayed…: Matthew chapters 26 and 27; Mark
chapters 14 to 15; Luke chapters 22 to 23; John chapters 18 to 19;
The Lord God…: Isaiah chapter 43, verses 1 and 2
p.39 Jesus died…: Luke chapter 23, verse 50 to chapter 24 verse 5;
As surely as seeds…: Isaiah chapter 61, verse 11
p.41 The Lord God said…: Ezekiel chapter 36, verse 24;
Get rid of…: Ephesians chapter 4, verses 22 to 24
p.43 In my special dream…: Revelation chapter 21

Introduction

Sometimes the world
seems a wonderful
place: a place of fun
and laughter, of beauty
and wonder,
of love and friendship.

Sometimes it seems cruel: a place of violence,
unfairness, tears, failure and desolation.

Where can hope be found? Is there anyone or
anything that can bind up the broken world
and make it right and good?

In this book are words and pictures to match
all these moods and open up the possibility of
faith in something greater than ourselves.

Contents

Joy and Wonder
A wonderful world

Every morning
the sun rises
on a new day.
There is so much
to enjoy,
so much
to make you
shout for joy.
Here are pictures
to remind you
of the good things
in the world.

The good earth

Here is cold, hard rock:
a strong foundation for the world.
Then the fiery sun warms it,
and the salt sea, the gentle rain
and the rushing wind
send it splitting, cracking, tumbling, crumbling
to make good earth.
These kind elements—
fire, water, air and earth
cradle the seeds
of all life.

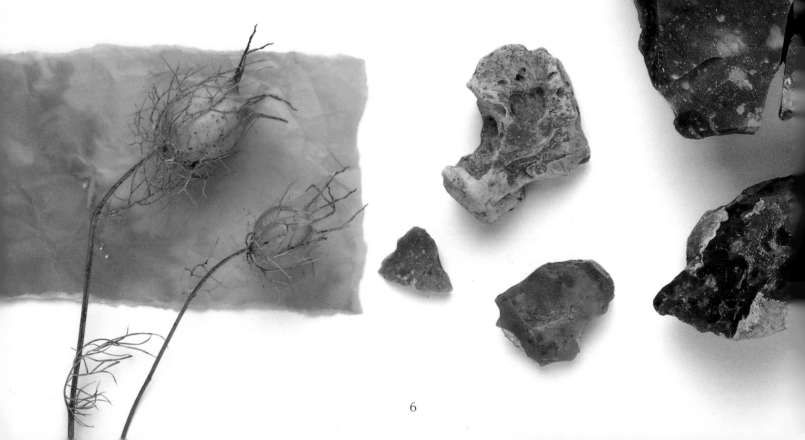

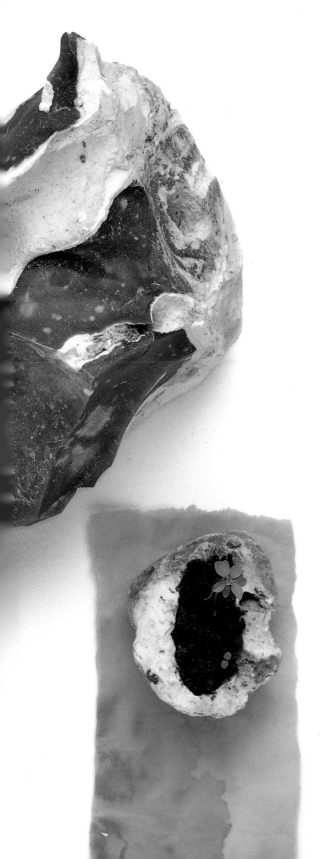

A great mystery

What holds up the pillars that support
the earth?
Who laid the cornerstone of the world?
Who laid the gates to hold back the sea?
Have you any idea how big the world is?
Answer me if you know.

God's questions to a man named Job,
from the book of Job, in the Bible.

A Christian gives his answer

Our God is the God of all,
The God of heaven and earth,
Of the sea and of the rivers;
The God of the sun and of the moon
and of all the stars;
The God of the lofty mountains
and of the lowly valleys.
He has his dwelling around heaven and
earth,
and sea, and all that in them is.

St Patrick

I wonder why the world
began, and I wonder why I
am alive in it.

7

Wildlife

Who had the wild idea
of making wildlife
and making it
look so wild
and wonderful—
all dressed up
for a wild and
wonderful party!

Look at the flowers

Jesus said,
'Look how the wild flowers grow: they do not work or make clothes for themselves. But I tell you that not even King Solomon with all his wealth had clothes as beautiful as one of these flowers. It is God who clothes the wild grass...'

Words of Jesus from the Gospel of Matthew, in the Bible

The world's song

Let the whole world praise the Lord
who made everything.
Praise the Lord, hills and mountains,
fruit-trees and forests;
all animals, tame and wild,
reptiles and birds.
Praise the Lord, all people everywhere...
girls and young men,
old people and children too.

From the book of Psalms, in the Bible

If you want to understand the Creator,
seek to understand created things.

Columbanus

Every part of me sings for joy at the wonders of the world.

Harvest

Feast your eyes
on harvest fruits!
By what magic,
by what miracle
do humble plants
turn sun and rain
into a rainbow
of food to eat?

A harvest song

O God, it is right for us to praise you.
You provide the earth with crops.
You send abundant rain on the
ploughed fields
and soak them with water;
you soften the soil with showers
and cause the young plants to grow.

From the book of Psalms, in the Bible

Sowe Carrets in your Gardens, and
humbly praise God for them, as for a
singular and great blessing.

Richard Gardiner From a 16th-century gardening book called *Profitable instructions for the manuring, sowing and planting of kitchen gardens* (1599)

The world gives us everything we need. I give thanks for the seasons and the harvest.

Clever me

Making things is fun.
And all it takes is
bits of this and that—
and clever ideas,
clever hands.

Glory

Oh, you gotta get a glory
In the work you do;
A Hallelujah chorus
In the heart of you.
Paint, or tell a story,
Sing, or shovel coal,
But you gotta get a glory,
Or the job lacks soul.
Anonymous

I take delight in all the clever things I can do.

Bless to me, O Lord,
the work of my hands.
Bless to me, O God,
the work of my mind.
Bless to me, O God,
the work of my heart.
Anonymous

Let the favour of the Lord our God
be upon us,
and prosper for us the work of our
hands—
O prosper the work of our hands!
From the book of Psalms, in the Bible

Home

A happy home
is snug with all the treasures
that remind you
of people who love you
and want the best for you.

One prayer only

Lord God,
I come to you
asking for just one thing:
I want to live in your house
all my life.
You will be good to me.
You will show me the right way to go.
You will take care of me.

From the book of Psalms, in the Bible

A thanksgiving to God

Lord, thou hast given me a cell
   Wherein to dwell;
A little house, whose humble roof
   Is weather-proof;
Under the spars of which I lie
Both soft and dry.

Robert Herrick (1591–1674)

I long to know that I am
loved just as I am.
I long to know that I am safe
in the world and for ever.

Sadness and Pain

A spoiled world

Sometimes when you look around the world
you find things that aren't wonderful.
You find that it isn't all fine.

The world can be cruel, harsh and painful.

Sometimes it makes you sad.

Sometimes it makes you angry.

Sometimes it makes you cry.

And surely it is right to rage
over the things that are wrong.

War

Here is the quarrel
you wouldn't end;
Here is the hate
that wounds a friend;
Here is anger,
here is spite,
here are the bullets
that flew all night;
Here are sharp words,
here are knives;
Here, the remains
of shattered lives.

Sing to us, Mama...
Mama, where are these killer birds from?
From far away, my love.
Mama, why do they come so many times?
They want to kill all of us, perhaps.
Why Mama?
I don't know, love; they are at war with us...
Mama, I'm scared.
Lovely, take your baby brother to a safer place
after the killer birds have flown away.
And you, Mama?
What about you?
I'm scared, Mama.
Mama! Mama! Mama!
Don't die, Mama!
Don't leave us alone, Mama!
Sing to us, Mama, so that we may cry together.
Mama! Mama! Mama! Mama!

Fan Yew Teng, Malaysia

18

Lord, make me an instrument of thy peace.
Where there is hatred, let me sow love.
Where there is injury, pardon.
Where there is discord, vision.
Where there is doubt, faith.
Where there is despair, hope.
Where there is darkness, light.
Where there is sadness, joy.

Anonymous, attributed to Francis of Assisi (1181–1226)

Jesus was speaking to the crowds.
'You all know this saying: "Love your friends;
hate your enemies." But now I am telling you
something different: love your enemies and pray
for those who deliberately hurt you.'

Words of Jesus from the Gospel of Matthew, in the Bible

I long for peace in the
world, both near and far.

Losers

It's not fair
that some win
and some lose.

It's not fair
that some have
and some have not.

Someone ought to put things right.

My Mother's Name is Worry

My mother's name is worry
In summer, my mother worries about water,
In winter, she worries about coal briquettes,
And all year long, she worries about rice.

In daytime, my mother worries about living,
At night, she worries for children.
And all day long, she worries and worries.

Then my mother's name is worry,
My father's is drunken frenzy,
And mine is tears and sighs.

Written by a twelve-year-old child in a slum area in Asia

I look at the high hills all around me and wonder,
'Where will my help come from?'
My help will come from the Lord,
the One who made heaven and earth.

From the book of Psalms, in the Bible

God says this:
I love what is fair.
I hate it when people put others down
and do all kinds of wrong things.

From the book of Isaiah, in the Bible

I want the world to be fair to me.
I want the world to be fair to everyone.

A trampled world

It is so easy to spoil the fragile
loveliness of the world.
But how can the world be mended?

God's Grandeur

The world is charged with the grandeur of
God.
It will flame out, like shining from shook foil;
It gathers to a greatness, like the ooze of oil
Crushed. Why do men then now not reck his
rod?
Generations have trod, have trod, have trod;
And all is seared with trade; bleared, smeared
with toil;
And wears man's smudge and shares man's
smell: the soil
Is bare now, nor can foot feel, being shod.

And for all this, nature is never spent;
There lives the dearest freshness deep down
things;
And though the last lights off the black
West went
Oh, morning, at the brown brink eastward,
springs—
Because the Holy Ghost over the bent
World broods with warm breast and with ah!
bright wings.

Gerard Manley Hopkins (1844–89)

Sadness

Sadness is an earth with
no sun, a tree with no leaves
and a bird with no song.

Laura Braithwaite

God asks a question

God asked, 'Can you shout orders to
the clouds and make them pour
with rain? Who is clever enough to
count the clouds and tilt them over
to pour out rain to bind the dust of
the earth into lumps of soil?'
And the man, Job, answered,
'Lord, I know you are stronger than
anything in the world.
You can do everything you want.
I thought I knew better.
But I was wrong.'

From the book of Job, in the Bible

I will walk gently in the world.

Who's to blame?

Sometimes
the person who spoils things
is me.

I don't always mean to.
It isn't my fault completely.
Yet in spite of all the excuses
it is me.

Dear God,
You are loving and forgiving.
Wash away all that is bad in me.
Make me clean.
Help me to do what is good and right.
Let me stay your friend.

From the book of Psalms, in the Bible

Jesus said, 'You can be sure of this. When
someone who has been doing wrong turns
back to God, heaven has its biggest parties.'

Words of Jesus from the Gospel of Luke, in the Bible

Jesus said, 'If you forgive others the wrongs
they have done to you, your
Father in heaven will also forgive you.'

Words of Jesus from the Gospel of Matthew, in the Bible

Forgive me, Lord, for thy dear Son,
The ill that I this day have done,
That with the world, myself, and thee,
I, ere I sleep, at peace may be.

Bishop T. Ken (1637–1711)

Sometimes I need forgiveness
and a fresh new start.

Death

Here is death.

Sea-washed white.
Frost-bitten black.
Mould-flecked decay.

Death is cold.
Death is lonely.
Death is an ending.

26

The prayer of a wanted man

Hear my prayer, O God;
Please help me,
Please don't turn away.
I am so, so worried
and so, so tired.
People hate me.
People are angry with me.
I'm scared of what they might do.
I'm terrified
and the terrors of death
crush me.

From the book of Psalms, in the Bible

My God, my God
Why have you abandoned me?

From the book of Psalms, in the Bible

As the rain hides the stars, as the
autumn mist hides the hills, as the clouds
veil the blue of the sky, so the dark
happenings of my lot hide the shining of
your face from me.

From a Gaelic prayer

When the dark is
all around me, I fear
it will last for ever.

Hope and Healing

Hope

When the world seems
dark
and sad
you long
for light
and life
and happiness.

Some things in the everyday world give hope in the dark
times: a promise of better things to come.

Some of these things are what remind people of their
faith in Jesus.

These people—Christians—believe Jesus is God, come to
earth as a person. They believe Jesus came to lift people
up from their sadness, and to welcome them to live as
God's friends, God's children.

Light in the dark

The tiny
flickering flame
of just one candle
scatters the deepest darkness.

Long ago, God made a promise to a nation who was suffering many troubles. 'One day,' God promised, 'a king will come to rescue you.'

The people who walked in darkness have seen a great light. They lived in a land of shadows, but now light is shining on them.
A child is born to us!
A son is given to us!
And he will be our ruler.
He will be called 'Wonderful Counsellor', 'Mighty God', 'Eternal Father', 'Prince of Peace'.

From the book of Isaiah, in the Bible

Many years later, a baby was born in that nation: Jesus. Many people came to believe that Jesus was the promised one.

Jesus said, 'I am the light of the world.'

Words of Jesus from the Gospel of John, in the Bible

Rise up, O flame:
By thy light burning,
Show to us beauty,
Wisdom and truth.

Christopher Praestorius (c.1600)

Dear God,
Light up my world
with your love.

Tireless love

When you are weary
and need someone to help,
who will do the kind deed
out of love alone?

Who will stoop down low enough
to wipe the dust off dirty feet
that are tired from walking
among stones and thorns?
Who will make weary people
feel clean and rested?

One evening, Jesus and his close friends met together for a special meal. Everyone was tired from the day. Who was going to do the servant's job, and wash everyone's dirty feet?

Jesus took the towel and a basin of water, and did the work himself.

He said, 'You know yourselves that I am your teacher and your leader, and I have chosen to be your servant. It is an example for you to follow: you must be willing to be servants to one another.

Here is a new commandment: love one another, as I have loved you.'

And Jesus also said, 'Peace is what I leave with you; it is my own peace that I give you.'

From the Gospel of John, in the Bible

Deep peace of the running wave to you,
Deep peace of the flowing air to you,
Deep peace of the quiet earth to you,
Deep peace of the shining stars to you,
Deep peace of the Son of Peace to you, for ever.

Anonymous

Dear God,
When I am weary, let me rest and know I am loved.

Bread and wine

Think how easily you can tear bread.
Think how easily a person's body can be
hurt and broken.

Think how easily a drink can be spilt.
Think how easily a person can be made
to bleed.

Think how hard it is
to undo the damage.

Jesus and the Last Supper

Jesus and his friends were sharing a special meal. Jesus took a piece of bread and said a prayer of thanks to God. Then he broke it into pieces and shared it with his friends. 'Take this and eat it,' he said. 'This is my body. It is going to be broken for you. And I want you to share bread in this way to remember me.'

After supper he took the cup of wine and held it for them to see. 'God is making a new agreement with people,' he said. 'You can be sure the agreement is real and true—my blood will be shed for it. I'm going to be killed, but I am dying for you.'

From the Gospels of Matthew, Mark and Luke, in the Bible

Dear God,
You let yourself be broken
so we could see
God's power to mend.

The Cross

Years of growing
have made wood lovely.
With one hammer blow
the sharp spike of a nail
marks it for ever.

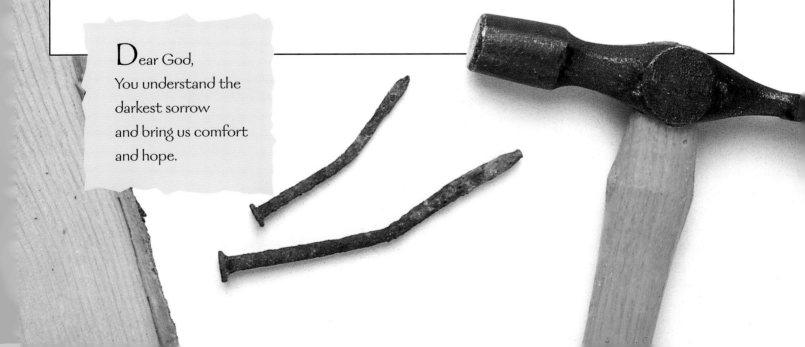

Jesus was betrayed by a friend
and handed over to those who
hated him.
They wanted nothing of his love
and kindness.
They wanted him dead.
They told lies about Jesus.
They said he was a troublemaker.
They had him put to death:
nailed to a cross of wood,
with spikes through his wrists
and feet—
crucified.

From the Gospels of Matthew, Mark, Luke and John, in the Bible

The Lord God says this:
'Do not be afraid.
I have come to save you.
You are special to me.
I know your name.
When the deep, dark waters of trouble
swirl around you,
I am with you.'

From the book of Isaiah, in the Bible

From the foot of the cross I look up to thee
O Jesus Lord bow down to me.
For I stand in the faith of my God today
Put love in my heart and hope alway.

Anonymous

Dear God,
You understand the
darkest sorrow
and bring us comfort
and hope.

New life

Springtime.
The light lingers
a little longer
in the evening sky.

Springtime.
Tiny seedlings
unfold green leaves
to the sun.

Springtime:
and the blossom
is like laughter
in the trees:

for the dead of winter
is defeated.

Jesus died on the cross.
Brave friends asked for his body
and they laid it in a tomb.
Three days later, very early,
when they went back to the tomb
its round stone door was open.
The body was gone.
Angels were there.
'Why are you looking among the dead
for one who is alive?' they asked. 'Jesus
is not here; he has been raised to life.'

From the Gospel of Luke, in the Bible

As surely as seeds sprout and grow,
God, who is in charge of all the world,
will put right every wrong.

From the book of Isaiah, in the Bible

God's promise of resurrection
is written not only in books
but in every springtime leaf.

Martin Luther (1483–1546)

Dear God,
I want to trust in your promise
of a new start—
a new life with you.

The sea

The sea is patient
and strong.
With every tide,
it washes smooth
the trampled sand.
With every tide,
it smooths
each jagged rock.
Every tide is a new beginning.

The Lord God said this:
'I will sprinkle clean water on you
and make you clean.
I will give you a new heart
and a new mind.
I will put my spirit in you
to enable you to live in the right way.'

From the book of Ezekiel, in the Bible

Get rid of your old self, and the wrongdoing
that made you feel so bad. You must put on
your new self, which is like God. This new you
does what is good and right.

From the letter to the Ephesians, in the Bible

God's mercy

God's boundless mercy is (to sinful man)
Like to the ever-wealthy ocean:
Which though it sends forth thousand streams,
'tis ne'er
Known, or else seen, to be the emptier;
And though it takes all in, 'tis yet no more
Full, and filled full, than when full filled before.

Robert Herrick (1591–1674)

Dear God,
Give me a new beginning
and help me become the
person I long to be.

A glimpse of heaven

One day
the rock
of this earth
will crumble away.
So what does 'for ever' mean?

In my special dream
I saw a new heaven
and a new earth.
The first heaven and the first earth
disappeared.
And I saw the Holy City coming down
out of heaven from God.
A voice spoke:
'Now God's home is with people. God
will be with them, and God will wipe
away their tears. There will be no more
death, no more grief or crying or pain.'
The city was of pure gold.
It shone with precious jewels.

And there was a river there, sparkling
with the water of life.
On each side of the river grew the tree
of life.
Its fruit gives life
and its leaves bring healing.

From the last book in the Bible, the book called Revelation

Lord, I am a countryman
    coming from my country to yours.
Teach me the laws of your country
    its way of life
    its spirit
So that I may feel at home there.

William de St Thierry (1085–1148)

Dear God,
I want to belong in your heaven
of peace and joy and love.

Index